I0489034

FUNDAMENTAL

CHURCH ADMINISTRATIVE
&
MINISTERIAL ETHICS

By

APELORIOYE I. DAVID

TABLE OF CONTENTS

DEDICATION

PREFACE

Chapter one
1. WHAT ARE ETHICS?

Chapter Two
2. CHURCH ADMINISTRATIVE ETHICS

Chapter Three
3. BASIC MINISTERIAL ETHICS

Chapter Four
4. ETHICS OF INVITING GUEST SPEAKERS.

Chapter Five
5. ETHICS OF PASTORS OVER CONGREGATIONS

Chapter Six
6. ETHICS OF A LEADING PASTOR AND ASSOCIATE/ASSISTING PASTORS

Chapter Seven
7. BOOK SUMMARY

Chapter Eight
8. SPIRIT INSPIRED QUOTES FROM THIS BOOK BY THE AUTHOR.

Chapter Nine
9. REVISION TESTS

Chapter Ten
10. PRAYER POINTS

DEDICATION

This church corrective and instructive manual **'Fundamental Church Administrative and Ministerial Ethics'** is dedicated to **PASTOR EZEKIEL ADEDOSU ODEYEMI**, the Assistant General Overseer (Education and Training) of the Redeemed Christian Church of God and Member of Governing Council of the Redeemer's University whose life has been a great blessing to me, who by the help of the Holy Spirit taught me Church Administration, Leadership in Ministry and Expository sermon during 1995/1996 Leadership Training for the Redeemed Christian Fellowship (RCF) Excos when I served as the Vice President/Evangelism Secretary of Owo Chapter, Ondo State, Nigeria.

Thank you Daddy, I am grateful sir!

CHAPTER ONE

ETHICS DEFINITIONS

Ethics refers to well-based standards of right and wrong that prescribe what humans ought to do, usually in terms of duties, principles, specific virtues, or benefits to society. In other words, ethics implies a broader range of expected behaviors and reflection about what should be done.

This definition identifies four dimensions or sources of ethics, one is based on the nature of public service while the other three are based on the philosophical perspectives to ethics:

1. *Duties*: The behaviors expected of persons who occupy certain roles; That is, the obligations taken on when assuming a role or profession

2. *Virtues*: Qualities that define what a good person is; that is moral excellence.

3. *Principles*: Fundamental truths that form the basis for behavior; "kinds of action that are right or obligatory" (Ethics: William K. Frankena 1963, 49)

4. *Benefits* to society: Actions that produce the greatest good for the greatest living.

The ethics in this book are set out very clearly in order to enhance our administrative and ministerial productivity. For persons who work in church as nonprofit organizations, duty has a special importance. They must serve the public, fulfill the expectations of public office, and be trustees of public resources. These are the actions required by their occupation or role independent of – but reinforced by – other ethical considerations.

When violation of moral standard of life is exhibited in any society, all we see is moral atrocity among the children, teenagers and adults. For example, moral misconducts cause series of hindrances to full life attainments such as;

1. Loss of value,
2. Loss of reputation,
3. Loss of focus,
4. Loss of direction
5. Abuse of nature
6. Loss of original identity and
7. Ultimately moral crashing.

> *There is a very high level of moral decadence in our society including the church offices and pulpits; the church is experiencing an ethical free fall because of the behavior of her leaders.*

There is a very high level of moral decadence in our society including the church offices and pulpits; the church is experiencing an ethical free fall because of the behavior of her leaders. This has become an embarrassment to all Christians. Administrative and

Ministerial Ethics addresses this issue and offers clear, candid, and comprehensive helps to both Pastors and church members.

CHAPTER TWO

CHURCH ADMINISTRATIVE ETHICS

If any church must be balanced and structured all-round administratively, certain principles and ideas as ethics must be inculcated in order to have formidable operations and output that would stand a test of time. Below are basic administrative ethics we will consider:

1. ETHICS OF CONFIDENTIALITY

A person with 'leaking mouth' (a talkative) should not be allowed to handle sensitive sections in church administration such as finance, audit, business arm of the church, committees, counseling and office administration jobs vis-à-vis promotion, query, transfer, minutes of Board Meeting etc. Even in the secular world where there are serious business competitions; rules of privacy are maintained among the staff.

When plans are still being formulated, though yet to be finalized or approved and the leaders or administrators divulge them,

> *When plans are still being formulated, though yet to be finalized or approved and the leaders or administrators divulge them, then there is no administration in such a place.*

then there is no administration in such a place.

Confidentiality of managerial decisions strengthens organization progress.

There are pastors members cannot talk to again on personal issues because such discussions will surface in the pastors' next sermon. In some churches, it's pastors' wives problem of divulging confidential information of members of the congregation. A pastor in ministry or an administrator who wants to excel should know how to control his/her mouth at all times.

A talebearer revealeth secrets: but he that is of a faithful spirit concealeth the matter. Proverb 11:13.

2. **ETHICS OF TRANSPARENCY**
   Openness or transparency in administration is a virtue that is missing in many churches today because of the shady deals of many church leaders. Imagine the situation where a church leader is all-in-all, he is the pastor, the treasurer, the cashier etc, telling people that he is very committed to the work of the Lord, is the reason for doing all for the Lord. It's either he/she is a novice or a thief. Whatever is being done in church administration should be

> *Openness or transparency in administration is a virtue that is missing in many churches today because of the shady deals of many church leaders.*

very clear to all the parties involved; how money is being generated and spent, how other assets being donated to the church are accounted for. Why should greed and love for material things carry pastors to hell?

3. **ETHICS OF CREATIVITY**
Creativity is not an option in moving things forward in ministry or in its administration. *A dull administrator or head of a church that cannot think fast or strategize church operations will only succeed in gathering dull people to himself.*

> *A dull administrator or head of a church that cannot think fast or strategize church operations will only succeed in gathering dull people to himself.*

Nothing is as painful as God is around to help His people by giving illuminative, tangible and result-oriented ideas, and the pastor or the administrator cannot discern that. Don't just allow your mind to be dull, the Holy Spirit is still in the business of imparting peoples' hearts with wisdom for everyone who asks.

One of the problems lack of creativity causes in the church administration is that it holds members on a spot, it blinds members or followers' eyes from seeing into the supernatural and it makes people suffer.

Until you are given to the reading of the word of God and fellowshipping with the Brethren who the Lord has illuminated their mind creatively and fellowshipping with the Spirit of the Lord, creativity in the things of God cannot come. Therefore, ask for wisdom today.

> *If any of you lack wisdom, let him ask of God, that giveth to all men liberally, and upbraideth not; and it shall be given him. James 1:5*

The same Spirit that rested on Jesus that made HIM exceptional can rest on you too if you are willing.

> *1: And there shall come forth a rod out of the stem of Jesse, and a Branch shall grow out of his roots:*
> *2: And the spirit of the LORD shall rest upon him, the spirit of wisdom and understanding, the spirit of counsel and might, the spirit of knowledge and of the fear of the LORD;*
> *3: And shall make him of quick understanding in the fear of the LORD: and he shall not judge after the sight of his eyes, neither reprove after the hearing of his ears: Isaiah 11:3*

Receive divine creativity in Jesus mighty name.

4. ETHICS OF ATTENDING TO MAILS REGULARLY

Whether electronic or hard copy mail, all mails should be responded to quickly as much as possible. There are organizations which have lost thousands and millions of Dollars just because an unserious and a negligent officer refused to treat mail as when due. Don't wait for your mails to turn to junk before they are treated. A good organization with right ethics responds to mail as early as possible. And every officer involved is told what to do. This also contributes to the goodwill of many organisations.

5. **ETHICS OF SINCERITY IN ALL THINGS**
Everyone in the administrative or accounting arm of the church should not be like Judas Iscariot who was greedy and heartless. In executing projects for the church, taking of bribe in whatever that's being done in the office is a serious offence in the Court of Heaven. For example, in some churches, pastors and workers manipulate and inflate figures when on official assignment to procure items for the church. Secular organisations frown at this, how much more about the church of God that supposed to be reputed as a holy place? Faithful and trustworthy persons should be employed into such offices.

Wherefore, brethren, look ye out among you seven men of honest report, full of the Holy

Ghost and wisdom, whom we may appoint over this business. Acts. 6:3

6. ETHICS OF PROPER PLANNING

The strength of any organization is ability to embark on strategic planning and execute it properly. Profiting, goodwill or failure in any organization lies within the organizational planning context. As the maxim says 'He who fails to plan has planned to fail'.

> *6: Go to the ant, thou sluggard; consider her ways, and be wise:*
> *7: Which having no guide, overseer, or ruler,*
> *8: Provideth her meat in the summer, and gathereth her food in the harvest. Proverb:6:8*

Nothing just happen on earth, they are planned and worked for. The emergence of large attendance in a church is not a function of pastor's unplanned life or fallen manna; they are planned and worked for. Every unprecedented encounter and breakthrough in ministry is birthed on the premise of proper planning in the will of God.

Even God is a great planner. In Genesis chapters 1 and 2, He planned what to do with the confused earth in a systematic and chronological order, He *Why must you not plan big when God is a great planner?* **began to unfold His plans daily and He got outstanding**

results. What He made the first day was not what He made the second day. If God planned to achieve His aim and put structures in place and ever since, plants reproduce its kinds every season, sun rises and sets every day, as a result we can count minutes, hours, days, weeks, months, years, decades, centuries and millenniums. Why must you not plan big when God is a great planner?

7. **ETHICS OF SEPARATION OF ACCOUNT (ENTITY CONCEPT)**

    Administrators who are Head Pastors or church leaders should not meddle with the church funds or make the mistakes of mixing their money with church money and accounts; everything should be separated in order to enhance proper accountability in all honesty. Churches are registered as Non Profit organisations, NGOs or as Charity and should not be run as a 'one man business' by her Trustees. In law, the church is a corporate soul while the pastors or trustees are human souls, there should be a clear distinction in accounts operated because church moneys are the peoples sweat and sacrificial penny given for the furtherance of the gospel. Pastors should not run church accounts as personal accounts, it is very detrimental to ministerial living.

    A Trustee is not the owner of the organization or trust

    > *Church moneys are the peoples sweat and sacrificial penny given for the furtherance of the gospel.*

property. An Incorporated Trustee is separate from and totally unrelated to the status of the individual Trustee(s) or member(s) either severally or collectively. In this regard note the following provisions of the Nigeria's Companies and Allied Matters Act 2004 which are produced hereunder for ease of reference

Section 603(1) *The income or property of a body or association whose trustee or trustees are incorporated under this part of the Act shall be applied solely towards the promotion of the objects of the body as set forth in its constitution and no portion thereof shall be transferred directly or indirectly by way of dividend, bonus or otherwise by way of profit to any of the members of the association*
608(4)

Trustee is not a position for "kill" and "divide". In other words, it is not a position for profit sharing as the Companies and Allied Matters Act 2004 in its section 603(1) prohibits the payment or transfer directly or indirectly by way of dividend, bonus or otherwise by way of profit to any of the members of the association of the income and property of the association or body whose Trustee(s) is/are Incorporated. It is for service unto the Lord.

In other nations like America, United Kingdom, Canada, Australia, South Africa etc, the provisions above are the same. In fact; the penalty for contravening them is stiffer and harsher than Nigeria's law. The day Nigeria Government wakes up to monitor Non Profit Bodies, many Registered Trustees of churches, Associations, Foundations etc may go to jail because of mismanagement and misappropriation of fund. Therefore, Trustee is not a position to exploit the Ministry or the beneficiaries.

8. ETHICS OF LEADING WITH VISIONARY APPROACH

Vision as Creative imagination and the mental capacity to construct the future one desires and make it a reality is an ethic that must be lived with in our churches. Everyone at the top of administrative or spiritual affairs is charged to be a visionary leader as Vision makes the difference between success and failure. **Pastor Ezekiel A. Odeyemi told us that 'a ministry or church without vision will soon become a mission field for other visionary ministries or churches to explore'.** Don't be a victim!

> *6: Go to the ant, thou sluggard; consider her ways, and be wise:*
> *7: Which having no guide, overseer, or ruler,*
> *8: Provideth her meat in the summer, and gathereth her food in the harvest. Proverb:6:8*

9. ETHICS OF DEPENDING ON THE HOLY SPIRIT FOR DIVINE WISDOM FOR OPERATION

Without wisdom which is the principal thing, every church leader or Administrator will fail very woefully. There are evils and subtle lifestyles of people emanating every day that divine wisdom can only tackle. Wisdom of God makes an ordinary man/woman do extraordinary things. It operates supernaturally natural in a man. Read Job 28:12-28

12: But where shall wisdom be found? and where is the place of understanding?
13: Man knoweth not the price thereof; neither is it found in the land of the living.
14: The depth saith, It is not in me: and the sea saith, It is not with me.
15: It cannot be gotten for gold, neither shall silver be *weighed for the price thereof.*
28: And unto man he said, Behold, the fear of the Lord, that is wisdom; and to depart from evil is understanding.

> Wisdom of God makes an ordinary man/woman do extraordinary things. It operates supernaturally natural in a man.

When wisdom of God is not in view in our church administrations, foolishness and stupid acts would be our watchwords and targets. Wisdom of God is a key to life.

10. ETHICS OF PROPER REPORTING

One thing that kills organization very easily is when everybody has access to the Chief Executive. Hierarchy or church organogram is not for fun, it is for orderliness and structural balance. Reporting is a way of making, analyzing the success and failure of the ministry in order to make proper adjustment for better efficiency. When a leader hears from too many people at the same time, he would be confused and no meaningful decision can be taken in the midst of confusion. Therefore, let the reporting policy be well structured so that the church would not be launched into chaos.

11. ETHICS OF OPERATING PROFESSIONALLY IN EVERY SPHERE

Every professional work in the church administration should be done professionally. That is, excellent service through professionalism. Vis-à-vis Administration, Accounting, Banking, Auditing, Legal services, Engineering, Medical etc. Professionalism enhances profitability (avoiding losses), promotes goodwill and growth of the organization. For example, an Engineer who downplays on the professional ethics of building may lose his license and incur great loss (loss of human, money and other valuable resources) for the church if the building collapsed.

From personal experience, I have discovered that church is an establishment where nearly everybody wants professionals to do things the way they like. This is wrong. As a pastor, Professional Accountant, Auditor and Administrator, I have been privileged to counsel many professionals in different fields in the church not to consent to peoples' '**shortcut**' because on the long run the people will rubbish their professionalism and their careers, and every layman will think they are foolish.

Listen, in the first instance why did the church engage your service as a professional? It's because you are needed. So, why would you compromise the standard and bring shame to yourself, other professionals and the name of our God?

My counsel to all professionals who God has called to serve in the church is that, instead of the church members and authorities to force you into shortcut that would have you being blamed at the end, resign from that work until the balance is struck, before the whole world would see you as a big fool. Therefore, **BE WISE!**

12. ETHICS OF PERIODIC ASSESSMENT OF THE MINISTRY AND ADMINISTRATIVE OPERATIONS

Periodic assessment of general operational strategies and base is a must in the church if we must move forward with salient performances and glorify God. Doing the same thing every year when there are lapses to correct is a sign that we hate the progress of the organization. All Departmental works and operations must be reviewed regularly. All church activities in the Board must be reviewed. In doing this, some people may be promoted while some demoted depending on the outcome of the review.
Also, before the review comes, suggestion box may be used to collect certain information which members may find difficult to tell the pastors and Board members directly when things are going wrong.

13. ETHICS OF ACCOUNTABILITY OF ALL DELEGATED AUTHORITY

It should be noted that a person to whom power or authority has been delegated cannot himself delegate such power or authority to another (delegatus non potest delegare). It should be noted also that the delegate remains responsible and accountable to the delegator. Every person saddled with certain responsibility should report back to the authority as we are accountable to God for the assignment He has given to us.

So then every one of us shall give account of himself to God. Rom.14:12

14. ETHICS OF SELF-DEVELOPMENT IN OFFICE OR PERSONAL DEVELOPMENT

Every employee should strive hard to develop themselves at work because church organizations may not be able to provide everything you need for your work, that is the reason some employees are more outstanding in every sphere at work than some because of quality time given to personal development programme. The good part is that every outstanding employee at work is rewarded by the employer.

> *Seest thou a man diligent in his business? he shall stand before kings; he shall not stand before mean men. Proverb 22:29.*

15. ETHICS OF MAINTAINING PROPER FILLING SYSTEM

Record keeping is a vital part of organization progress. We have the Holy Bible today because of its preservation. When records are lost or missed up easily in any organization is a way to slow down the progress as no meaningful decisions can be made without records at hand. Every filling system either manual or computerized should be well coded and organized in order to meet the decision of the organization. These are some of the records which should be kept very well.

- a. Finance
- b. Personnel
- c. Transfer of pastors
- d. Promotion, track records
- e. Queries issued
- f. Church Assets
- g. Other inter-organisational correspondence.
- h. Meetings procedures and follow up all board's decisions arrived at.

Everybody in the organization should not have access to the record pool, safe the authorized personnel as it will be very easy to know who to hold responsible.

16. ETHICS OF NOT SKIPPING DISCIPLINARY ACTIONS FOR ANYBODY

Discipline either from God or man is one of the actions that sustain the church. As much as possible in the church, nobody should be a 'sacred cow' or tagged 'the untouchable' to thwart Disciplinary Committee (DC) decisions. Nobody should be shielded by any Power Brokers from being exposed to disciplinary actions as much as we want our local assemblies

> *As much as possible in the church, nobody should be a 'sacred cow' or tagged 'the untouchable' to thwart Disciplinary Committee (DC) decisions.*

and the Body of Christ to grow in every good sphere.

When a bad legacy is laid, it will become bad precedents or premonition to the church which would affect the next generations adversely.

Therefore, everybody in the church administration should not be self-centered or selfish so that we would not bring up half-baked Christians for the Lord who would come and turn upside-down the good work we have done for the Lord.

Them that sin rebuke before all, that others also may fear. 1Tim. 5:20

> If you don't train them, don't blame them.

17. ETHICS OF PROVIDING REGULAR TRAINING FOR OFFICE STAFF

This is to enhance Staff effectiveness, versatility, responsibilities, and official delivery. A popular maxim says **'If you don't train them, don't blame them'.** Every ministry should train her staff regularly either in-house training or external training. It will bring more yields to the church performance. If people in the other religions and in the Terrorist world can spend millions of dollars to advance their evil course in training their own; how much more the church of God which have a focus and Kingdom goals at heart? The following areas should be considered regularly for training:

Pastors for conferences
Children Teachers
Teenagers Teachers
Security Department
Ushering Department
Protocol Department
Audit department
Accounts Department
Admin Department
Media Department
Technical Department
Evangelism Department
Prayer Band etc.

Good and regular training preserve legacy for the unborn generations and raise faithful and committed disciples for Jesus.

18. ETHICS OF LEADING WITH EXAMPLES

A church Pastor or an administrative senior staff who is stealing money or manipulating financial and attendance figures, how can he or she lead well? It is very difficult. The ethics of leading the church with the leadership of good example must be upheld because we are the Bible the people read to live their lives. As a church leader, your actions should not lead the young ones to hell. There are church members who have said they won't go to the church again because of the pastors' bad lifestyles. This is a thing of shame. Therefore, the ethics of top management leaving a very good legacy for the Junior staff should be upheld at all times.

For I have given you an example, that ye should do as I have done to you. John 13:15

Let no man despise thy youth; but be thou an example of the believers, in word, in conversation, in charity, in spirit, in faith, in purity. 1Tim. 4:12

19. ETHICS OF DELEGATING AUTHORITY PROPERLY AND THE ACCOMPANIED   RESPONSIBILITIES
Delegation is good but delegating rightly is better. This ethics must be adhered to if we must make it in the practice of Church Administration. It is not enough to delegate, but delegate the entirety of the work to be done properly by showing them step by step as Priest Jethro told Prophet Moses to do the leaders to be appointed in Israel.

> *19: Hearken now unto my voice, I will give thee counsel, and God shall be with thee: Be thou for the people to Godward, that thou mayest bring the causes unto God:*
> *20: And thou shalt teach them ordinances and laws, and shalt shew them the way wherein they must walk, and the work that they must do.*

21: *Moreover thou shalt provide out of all the people able men, such as fear God, men of truth, hating covetousness; and place such over them, to be rulers of thousands, and rulers of hundreds, rulers of fifties, and rulers of tens:*

22: *And let them judge the people at all seasons: and it shall be, that every great matter they shall bring unto thee, but every small matter they shall judge: so shall it be easier for thyself, and they shall bear the burden with thee. Exodus 18:18-21*

Jethro was an administrator and a priest. He counseled Moses further thus: "Thou wilt surely wear away, both thou, and this people that is with thee: for this thing is too heavy for thee; thou art not able to perform it thyself alone".

Many ministers of the gospel died early because they don't delegate with the fear that the person whom he/she delegate assignments to would outshine him/her.

20. ETHICS OF NOT OWING STAFF MONTHLY SALARY AND OTHER ALLOWANCES

Many ministers of the gospel died early because they don't delegate with the fear that the person whom he/she delegate assignments to would outshine him/her.

There are Ministries or Churches where those in authorities are cruising and enjoying life while their employees are languishing in hunger, poverty and sorrows of heart because of unpaid salaries and wages duly worked for. God hates this! It is an abomination in His sight! Here what the Bible says below:

> *For the scripture saith, Thou shalt not muzzle the ox that treadeth out the corn. And, the labourer is worthy of his reward. 1Tim. 5:18.*

> *He that oppresseth the poor reproacheth his Maker: but he that honoureth him hath mercy on the poor. Proverbs 14:31*

> *He that oppresseth the poor to increase his riches, and he that giveth to the rich, shall surely come to want. Proverbs 22:16.*

Every pastor and administrator at the helm of affairs should be very careful in this regard so that they would not go back to the state they were before they became rich.
Therefore, don't employ numbers of staff you cannot pay and don't owe the ones you have already employed.

21. ETHICS OF FOLLOWING HIERARCHY IN ORDER TO GET THE ORGANIZATION STRUCTURE STRAIGHT

Order is the mother of progress. Organization structure or hierarchical order is not for fun, it is for structural balance. Therefore, utmost importance needs to be attached to them. Every officer should follow the line of communication in order to avoid bottleneck in the administrative proceedings. Junior staff should not jump reporting through his immediate superior who is a middle level management to report to the top management because of familiarity in the system. Nothing kills system easily like everybody having access to the Chief Executive.

For yourselves know how ye ought to follow us: for we behaved not ourselves disorderly among you; 2Thess. 3:7

Let all things be done decently and in order. 1Cor. 14:40

> Order is the mother of progress. Organization structure or hierarchical order is not for fun, it is for structural balance.

This is one of the reasons why policies of the church should be well documented and followed properly. This can cost any ministry goodwill, orderliness and progress.

22. ETHICS OF AVOIDING CHURCH POLITICS
As at today in any part of the world there is no place where evil is not attached to the game of

politics because of the nature of the hearts of men; being in schools or at any level of government or in churches or at home. Remember that evil is evil. In other words, there is no good part of evil.

What is not right is wrong. Church politics should not be brand-named or garnished with all kinds of false vocabularies. It is a wrong act, and it takes sound spirituality to avoid church politics.

14: Enter not into the path of the wicked, and go not in the way of evil men.
15: Avoid it, pass not by it, turn from it, and pass away. Proverb:4:14-15.

Politics in the church is all about pulling one down politically and raising one up unjustly. This should be avoided. Many young ministers pastoral career have been delayed or destroyed because of godfathers' influence especially when the younger pastors concerned are not bringing "seed, venison or envelops" as it should be.

In some churches or ministries, many pastors who have done excellently well with proven track of records in expansion and evangelism are posted to villages while those who ought to be demoted because they are found wanting in their personal and family life are enjoying blissful posting because they have settled the top with **"seed, venison or envelops"**. This is oppression. Avoid it!

You can read more about church politics in my book *"Church politics, the killer of great grace"*.

23. ETHICS OF REGARDING THE GOVERNMENTAL LAWS IN OPERATING THE CHURCH

The church cannot operate alone without having anything to do with the government of the land. Certain governmental regulations should be adhered to in order to get the best of the operations of the church. These are: registrations to enable the church enjoy corporate soul benefits, filling of annual returns to the relevant authorities, staff income tax return.

> *1: Let every soul be subject unto the higher powers. For there is no power but of God: the powers that be are ordained of God.*
> *2: Whosoever therefore resisteth the power, resisteth the ordinance of God: and they that resist shall receive to themselves damnation. Rom.13:1-2*

However, this should EXCLUDE other governmental regulations in some nations which are against the Bible such as enacting homosexual, lesbianism, adultery, bestiality, incest into law. It is satanic, unethical, barbaric and unacceptable to the highest Government-HEAVEN.

Beloved, follow not that which is evil, but that which is good. He that doeth good is of God: but he that doeth evil hath not seen God. 3John 1:11

24. ETHICS OF STUDYING AND KNOWING CHURCH HISTORY

History can always repeat itself in either negative or positive ways depending on what one knows about them. I encourage every church leader to study history along with the laws guiding their works, health issues and basic administration of the church. One of the reasons church leaders or administrators of the past decades and the contemporary age fail is because they don't study history of those who have gone before them. So, they fell into the same errors those ahead of them fell into.

I read through the book God's Generals by Roberts Liardon and I discovered that some of them died prematurely despite the level of outstanding manifestations of the power of God in ministry. Why? The answer lies in lack of effective delegation. They did everything in ministry-both the spiritual and administrative duties themselves and in the process failed to create adequate time to fellowship with the Holy Spirit. Some of them died in errors and some died of the sickness they were once given power to cast out. Some expired early because of competition in ministry and thereby lost focus. Majority of them died because of unnecessary and avoidable stress.

25. ETHICS OF STUDYING THE REASONS PEOPLE LEAVE THE CHURCH

This involves what to do to satisfy the congregations' needs. Serious minded people as church members walk away from visionless pastors and Administrators. When a Pastor has no vision, those under him do not know where they are going. They do not understand the plan and pursuit of the ministry per time. And a Pastor who does not make his vision plain is confused and can be directed anyhow. The backdoor is enforced when needs are not met. When members keep coming to Church and their needs are not met, they will look for somewhere else to go to.

People also walk out of Churches where there is no love and affection.

> *2: And the LORD answered me, and said, Write the vision, and make it plain upon tables, that he may run that readeth it.*
>
> *3: For the vision is yet for an appointed time, but at the end it shall speak, and not lie: though it tarry, wait for it; because it will surely come, it will not tarry. Hab. 2:3*

I have heard pastors who told the congregation that anyone who wants to leave the church should leave, that they will beg to come back. Sir, it is not true. God is in some ministries more than your own; that people are coming to fellowship with you is a privilege. Don't misuse it.

> Serious minded people as church members walk away from visionless pastors and Administrators.

26. ETHICS OF APPRECIATING PASTORS FOR THEIR GOOD WORKS

Setting out a time or a day in certain period to honour pastors is not out of place. By the word pastors, I mean any ministry office that leads souls such as prophets, apostles, Evangelist, bishops, a teacher or a pastor. Doing this for a man of God is doing this for God.

> *41: He that receiveth a prophet in the name of a prophet shall receive a prophet's reward; and he that receiveth a righteous man in the name of a righteous man shall receive a righteous man's reward.*
>
> *42: And whosoever shall give to drink unto one of these little ones a cup of cold water only in the name of a disciple, verily I say unto you, he shall in no wise lose his reward. Matthew 10:41-42.*

When the congregation honours their pastors, they are also honouring God in heaven. The church should not wait till a pastor dies before they give him posthumous (after death) honour of buying

> *When the congregation honours their pastors, they are also honouring God in heaven.*

one Million Dollar casket, while he suffered of hunger before death. Church is reputed to be a 'going concern' but pastors are not. Honour them now!

27. ETHICS OF PREPARING FOR STAFFS RETIREMENT

Retirement benefit is one thing that alleviates pastors suffering after retirement when there is not much to fall back on. That may come in the form of Pension and gratuity which need to be worked towards and should be put into consideration or having personal investments such as giving quality training to their children and having businesses. Church employees either as administrative staff or fulltime pastors should be considered for Pension and gratuity as one of the church policies.

To get this done, right pension contributory system needs to be adopted and the right choice of pension administrators.

So teach us to number our days, that we
may apply our hearts unto wisdom. Psalms
90:12

28. ETHICS OF TIME MANAGEMENT IN ALL WE DO

In whatever we do either in the church services or in the offices, we should be time conscious. Let consider the following quotes.

"Make use of time, let not advantage slip" by William Shakespeare.

"Time is the raw material that processes destiny" by *Apostle Prof. Johnson Suleman.*

"A man who dares to waste one hour of life has not discovered the value of life" by Charles Darwin.

"Dost thou love life? Then do not squander time, for that is the stuff life is made of" by Benjamin Franklin.

"Time is money" by Benjamin Franklin.

"God gave all of us twenty four (24) hour every day, seven (7) days every week, four (4) weeks every month, twelve months (12) every year. What you do with your time depends on what your time will do to you" by Apelorioye I. David (Book author)

"Those who achieve success, respect and honor time in their ministry and personal life" by Apelorioye I. David (Book author)

29. ETHICS OF DISAGREEING WITH THE SPIRIT OF ABSALOM IN THE CHURCH (REBELLION)

Rebellion in church administration or church setting as a whole is evil and it's against the will of God. Rebellion against constituted authorities is sin. It should not be tolerated or condoned in any level.

> *For rebellion is as the sin of witchcraft, and stubbornness is as iniquity and idolatry. Because thou hast rejected the word of the LORD, he hath also rejected thee from being king. 1Sam. 15:23*

Rebellion should be summoned as early as possible so that it would not grow to develop tentacles for evil practices in the church.
You can read more about this in my book *"The Ministry of Assistant and Associate Pastors.*

30. ETHICS OF FUND-RAISING

Ethic of fund-raising for the church should be distinct from the manipulative fund-raising that many church leaders go into in order to make money for themselves. *What is needed in the church should be what to raise fund for and should be well accounted for.*

> *Pastors should not hide under raising fund for church needs to raise fund for themselves, it's wrong*

Do not raise money to procure speaker and use it

for other expenses, it will amount to misappropriation. The congregation will not trust the pastors again except he carries everybody along. If you want to raise money to help the pastor's personal needs, make it very clear to the people; pastors should not hide under raising fund for church needs to raise fund for themselves, it's wrong. Let's look at what happened when Israel was building the temple in Exodus 36:2-7

> *2: And Moses called Bezaleel and Aholiab, and every wise hearted man, in whose heart the LORD had put wisdom, even every one whose heart stirred him up to come unto the work to do it:*
> *3: And they received of Moses all the offering, which the children of Israel had brought for the work of the service of the sanctuary, to make it withal. And they brought yet unto him free offerings every morning.*
> *4: And all the wise men, that wrought all the work of the sanctuary, came every man from his work which they made;*
> *5: And they spake unto Moses, saying, The people bring much more than enough for the service of the work, which the LORD commanded to make.*
> *6: And Moses gave commandment, and they caused it to be proclaimed throughout the camp, saying, Let neither man nor woman make any more work for the offering of the*

sanctuary. So the people were restrained from bringing.
7: For the stuff they had was sufficient for all the work to make it, and too much.

This is a good example of what fund-raising in our churches should be. The offerings they brought was used for the exact work and when they had enough, Moses the senior pastor of the congregation gave a commandment for people to stop bringing more offerings for that purpose. Some pastors or administrators of today world would have diverted those excess materials brought to build their personal houses.

> *For we brought nothing into this world, and it is certain we can carry nothing out. 1Tm:6:7*

You can read more about this in my book **"Effective Church Administration,** *the making of the Holy Spirit".*

31. ETHICS OF NOT WORKING IN THE CHURCH BECAUSE OF MONEY

Church work is divinely controlled. Your aim of entering into ministry or church work should not be to make money or amass wealth. Jesus said in

Matthew 6: 33-34:

*33: But seek ye FIRST the kingdom of God,
and his righteousness; and all these
things shall be added unto you.*

*34: Take therefore no thought for the morrow:
for the morrow shall take thought for the
things of itself. Sufficient unto the day is
the evil thereof.*

Money should not be the reason why you want to work in the church or reason you would like to be in control.

Paul the Apostle was talking to the Christian of old in 1Tim:6:10-11 that "For the love of money is the root of all evil: which while some coveted after, they have erred from the faith, and pierced themselves through with many sorrows. But thou, **O man of God,** flee these things; and follow after righteousness, godliness, faith, love, patience, meekness".

32. ETHICS OF TAKING REST WHEN THE NEED ARISES IN ORDER TO WORK MORE FOR THE DAYS AHEAD

Rest is medicinal. Rest is good health advocator. Rest is preparing for better work tomorrow. Rest is godly when the

> *Rest is medicinal. Rest is good health advocator. Rest is preparing for better work tomorrow.*

need arises. Take a good rest after work so that

you can be at alert in thinking and meditation. From personal experience, I discovered that when one is stressed, official delivery will become very low and it will reduce one's ability to pray and hear from God.

The following signal of stress Insomnia, Migraine and headache, isolation, Loss of appetite, Sighing, Boredom, and Tiredness may lead to other complicated issues if not handled early.

Stress is interconnected with the topmost causes of death globally; accident, heart diseases.

Stress is a silent killer which causes chest pain, high cholesterol, cardiac (heart) problems, depression etc.

Stress can change the temperament of gentle pastors as misplaced anger, and aggressions may be the results. And Stress makes one looks older than his or her age.

33. ETHICS OF USING THE BEST HAND TO LEAD THE ORGANIZATIONAL ROLES

This ethic is what gives the best to the church administration as the best hands are used for every

> *Stress can change the temperament of gentle pastors as misplaced anger, and aggressions may be the results.*

assignment while others would be learning to gain mastery and capacity for subsequent assignments. Politics should not come into this so that the church would not suffer loss.

Personally, I believe in professionalism and spirituality in every sphere. Even king David of Old manifested skills and spirituality. Don't put a novice in the position of a professional. It's a big risk.

Sing unto him a new song; play skillfully with a loud noise. Psalm 33:3

Imagine someone because of his loyalty to authority with only theology credentials who has never worked in secular places of administration or leadership to head administration of a church; and is employed as church administrator or accountant especially in a big church, he/she will fail woefully. Skillful people are needed to get good results in the church.

34. ETHICS OF HANDLING CHURCH CONFLICTS AS EARLY AS POSSIBLE SO THAT IT WON'T DEGENERATE INTO CRISIS

Church conflicts either at the departmental level or branch level should be handled with care and very early as much as possible. I have seen in some ministries where conflicts not well managed at the Management Level metamorphosed into crises which led to serious injuries and the death of many because physical assaults were involved.

In other ministries, members go beyond the physical realm to employ strange demonic powers against themselves. It shows that they are not born again in the first instance. All these ought not to happen at all because the Body of Christ is reputed for unity which is the hallmark of great success in life.

> *For God is not the author of confusion, but of peace, as in all churches of the saints. 1Cor. 14:33.*

35. ETHICS OF CHECKS AND BALANCES

As much as possible, no administrative staff should begin a transaction and end it as the rules of accounting internal control does not permit that. There should be due measure of control put in place; this has made some churches suffered several embezzlements, errors in recording and pilfering because trust is concentrated on one person. Checks and balances are not a sign of hatred or sentimental display of distrust but it has been the

> *Checks and balances are not a sign of hatred or sentimental display of distrust but it has been the principle of achieving the best for every organization*

principle of achieving the best for every organization.

For example, that your biological brother is a bank manager or cashier does not mean that he would just give you money without checking your account balance, date, amount, signatures, etc in your cheque book. Ethics of checks and balances apply so that he would not incur liability. So it is in the church.

36. ETHIC OF PREPARING MEETING AGENDA BEFORE IT HOLDS

Churches or Organizations who have nothing reasonable to discuss should not hold meeting at all or when agenda isn't in place. This is one of the ways time and valuable resources are wasted; when there is nothing special in view. It's ethical to prepare adequately for every meeting before it holds as any time wasted may not be recovered easily.

So teach us to number our days, that we may apply our hearts unto wisdom. Psalm 90:12

37. ETHIC OF COUNSELING WITHOUT BEING BIAS OR SENTIMENTAL

Counseling is one of the sensitive areas of the church administration and ministering. When you are counseling, don't take side with any party so that your ministry of counseling would not be abused. Also, during counseling, if there is any question you cannot answer, tell them to contact you later for answer. Don't be a superman counselor who fails before novice counselees because of saying what you don't know.

On the other hand, due diligence should be exercised when you are counseling opposite sex because must sexual scandals and abuses in ministry emanated from counseling period when intimate personal talks are discussed. As a church leader or an administrator, when you are counseling and it is tilting towards wrong directions or arousing your sexual passion, please stop it

> *Don't be a superman counselor who fails before novice counselees because of saying what you don't know.*

immediately so that COUNSELING won't CANCEL you out of ministry, and cry to God for virtue of self-control.

CHAPTER THREE

BASIC MINISTERIAL ETHICS

Some of the administrative ethics mentioned above also form part of ministerial ethics which we will be looking at since all is about church that every church leader needs to succeed.

1. **ETHICS OF FOCUS**

   Ministry is full of troubles and distractions because we are in the very dark world of evil as 1John 5:19 says that *"And we know that we are of God, and the whole world lieth in wickedness"*. Because the whole world lies in wickedness, co-pastors will give you problems, church workers will give you problem, world of darkness (marine, witchcraft, diabolic etc) will give you problem especially if you are making serious imparts in the Holy Ghost. False allegations and scandals would be orchestrated against you if you are called and genuine. There are hundreds of issues that would declare you a sad man/woman everyday **BUT STAY FOCUSED!**

   > *Focus is what guarantees your next success and achievement in ministry despite all odds.*

Focus is what guarantees your next success and achievement in ministry despite all odds. No matter what you see, rejoice in the Lord always so that you can cause others to be joyful also.

2. ETHICS OF TRUTHFULNESS OF THE MESSAGES PREACHED

Your message should not be targeted towards certain set in the church, may be they didn't give you money as rich men and women or give you enough accolades. Remember that true and lasting honour comes from the Lord.

> *I receive not honour from men. John 5:41*

> *Jesus answered, If I honour myself, my honour is nothing: it is my Father that honoureth me; of whom ye say, that he is your God. John 8:54*

Situational messages to impress people should not be preached but as the Holy Spirit leads since ministry is all about the Holy Spirit and His work in Christ Jesus.

> *And my speech and my preaching was not with enticing words of man's wisdom, but in demonstration of the Spirit and of power 1Cor. 2:4*

3. ETHICS OF MINISTERING WITHOUT GREED

Greed is eating one's tomorrow today. Greed is one of the vices that have stopped many ministers of the gospel untimely in ministry. They want to have all things at the same time thereby putting hands into wrong things and make shipwreck of their ministries.

He that is greedy of gain troubleth his own house; but he that hateth gifts shall live. Proverb 15:27

This also involves raising money for oneself or billing the church on invitation before it is honoured. Jesus said freely you have received, give freely Matthew10:8.

4. ETHICS OF COMPETENCE

Ministering is not for baby in Christ, every minister called into ministering should be trained properly before climbing pulpits; competent ministers and not a novice or baby in the Lord. Even Apostle Paul stayed for sometimes under training with other disciples and Barnabas for learning after conversion. Acts 9:19,27, Gal. 2:1. Nineteen years ago, in the church I was then as a minister, two men

> *Greed is eating one's tomorrow today.*

were invited to minister in the church programme, they weren't composed at all, so mechanical on the altar, they didn't do well because of personal misbehavior; and were even trying to query God by amplifying their failure publicly. At the end of the meeting, I met our Pastor, and I asked, "Sir, where did you see these men?" He replied, "my brother, I was very shocked also". Use competent hands to do the best job for all. Others can be trained until they are matured to lead others. This also connect ethic 33 above.

> *6: Not a novice, lest being lifted up with pride he fall into the condemnation of the devil.*
> *7: Moreover he must have a good report of them which are without; lest he fall into reproach and the snare of the devil. 1Tim. 3:6-7*

5. ETHICS OF DEPENDING ON THE HOLY GOD FOR THE MINISTERIAL ESTABLISHMENT

Ministry must be done with Holy Bible Curriculum, it is the work of the Holy God that must be done by holy people in the holy way. This is an ethic of following Biblical principles as scriptures do not have private interpretations.

> *15: But as he which hath called you is holy, so be ye holy in all manner of conversation;*
> *16: Because it is written, Be ye holy; for I am holy. 1Pet. 1:15-16*

You cannot help God in ministry! Other religions help their gods but in Christianity, our God helps us. Do you want to perform miracles in ministry? It must be done by God's Spirit alone! Do you want to have crowd in ministry? It must be done by God's Spirit alone. Are you clamoring for fame or honour in ministry? It must be done by God's Spirit alone! If the Holy God is not the one doing it, then it is capitally faked. Every ministry success must be by the Spirit of God!

In all thy ways acknowledge him, and he shall direct thy paths. Proverb 3:6

6. DON'T GO INTO THE MINISTRY YOU DON'T HAVE CAPACITY AND GRACE FOR

Division of labour in Ministry is standing in your office divinely given. Therefore, doing ministry you don't have capacity and grace for is an act of pride and is the roadmap to ministerial failure. Therefore, stay in your calling. Even the Lord who gave some five talents, two talents and one talent knows what He is doing. Imagine a prophet doing the work of teacher when the grace is not there or a teacher doing the work of an Apostle when such ministry is nor given to him, they will only fail woefully and that itself is an act of pride. This has made several minsters of

> *You cannot help God in ministry! Other religions help their gods but in Christianity, our God helps us.*

the gospel go into all kinds of blunders and profanities because of doing what they don't have grace for. Please, read and meditate on Ephesians 4:11-14 below:

> 14: *And he gave some, apostles; and some, prophets; and some, evangelists; and some, pastors and teachers;*
> 12: *For the perfecting of the saints, for the work of the ministry, for the edifying of the body of Christ:*
> 13: *Till we all come in the unity of the faith, and of the knowledge of the Son of God, unto a perfect man, unto the measure of the stature of the fullness of Christ:*
> 14: *That we henceforth be no more children, tossed to and fro, and carried about with every wind of doctrine, by the sleight of men, and cunning craftiness, whereby they lie in wait to deceive;*

You can ask the Lord to give you any ministry gift you like, and wait for it to come so that you will not lead multitude astray.

7. ETHICS OF ADEQUATE PREPARATION BEFORE PREACHING OR TEACHING

Ministry is one of the places I have seen pastors ministering without adequate preparation. Late hour to enter pulpit, you see them carrying Concordance to look for references, this is not good enough. We know that it is the work of the Spirit but at the time human involvement are essential is in the place of prayers and study. **As the saying goes 'prayerful preparation prevents poor performance, or prayerful preparation promotes good performance.**

> *Study to shew thyself approved unto God, a workman that needeth not to be ashamed, rightly dividing the word of truth. 2Tim. 2:15*

Ministry is not for lazy people. It requires hard and wise work. There are people listening to you for the first time that may not see you again in life; they should be blessed as a result of adequate preparations. Don't gamble with ministry!

8. **ETHIC OF LIVING IN HARMONY WITH AND AMONG CO-MINISTERS**
Jesus said in Gospel according to St. John13:35 that 'By

> *Doing ministry you don't have capacity and grace for is an act of pride and is the roadmap to ministerial failure.*

this shall all men know that ye are my disciples, if ye have love one to another'. One major thing that glorifies Jesus is unity of brethren. Therefore, every minister should live in harmony no matter the denomination you belong to since we are bought with the same precious blood of Jesus.

*1: Behold, how good and how pleasant it is
for brethren to dwell together in unity!*
*2: It is like the precious ointment upon the
head, that ran down upon the beard,
even Aaron's beard: that went down to
the skirts of his garments;*
*3: As the dew of Hermon, and as the dew
that descended upon the mountains of
Zion: for there the LORD commanded
the blessing, even life for evermore.
Psalm133: 1-3.*

From the scripture above, it means in the unity of brethren, there are blessings.

9. ETHICS OF ACCOUNTABILITY

Every minister of the Gospel must and should know that they are accountable for every decision or action made in the course of ministering. Firstly, you are accountable to God, secondly, to the Board/Committees/Senior Ministers as the case may be, and thirdly, you are accountable to the government of the land. The end product of accountability depends on either you would be praised or blamed for all initial actions and decisions. Many pastors have ended their calling in prisons not because of persecution for Jesus Christ but as a result of false dealings discovered by the higher authorities. In whatever you are doing, know that you are accountable.

So then every one of us shall give account
of himself to God. Rom. 14:12

10. ETHICS OF GIVING RESPECT TO THOSE WHO ARE AHEAD IN MINISTRY

One thing that is missing among the young ministers of today is that most of them don't know those who are ahead of them in ministry. That all of us can preach or prophesy or teach or work miracles does not mean that we are all at the same ministerial rank or level. Know those who entered ministry before you no matter the grace you are enjoying and know those who are older than you so that ministry would not be abused.

> *That every one of you should know how to*
> *possess his vessel in sanctification and*
> *honour; 1Thess. 4:4*

11. ETHICS OF COMMENDING OR LIFTING ONE ANOTHER UP PUBLICLY

No matter how good you are in ministry, see others better than yourself. This is humility. God is the giver of grace, when you begin to see yourself better than others, you won't value anybody again and you won't go far in life. And the truth is that there are people far better than you in ministry, who have what you don't have no matter the year you have spent in ministry. Let us celebrate and honour ourselves before the Lord. This is love and practical humility.

> **24: And let us consider one another to provoke unto love and to good works:**
> **25: Not forsaking the assembling of ourselves together, as the manner of some is; but exhorting one another: and so much the more, as ye see the day approaching. Heb. 10:24-25.**

The church should pray for this kind of heart from the Lord

> *No matter how good you are in ministry, see others better than yourself.*

regularly. It is then we can call on ourselves for prayers and study of the word. No man has all about ministry.

12. ETHICS OF HELPING ONE ANOTHER IN TIME OF TROUBLE

This is a generation where nearly everyone looks for his own thing without putting others into consideration. We are in the era where the challenge or problem encountered by a minister makes other ministers to celebrate instead of interceding for them. This is another way of saying the church is indirectly glorifying the devil with the ungodly characters exhibited.

1: Brethren, if a man be overtaken in a fault, ye which are spiritual, restore such an one in the spirit of meekness; considering thyself, lest thou also be tempted.
2: Bear ye one another's burdens, and so fulfil the law of Christ. Gal. 6:1-2

Let us love indeed. Love is the greatest and God is love. 1 Cor. 13:1-3

If you mock others in trouble, when your trouble comes Satan will also hire someone greater to mock you; because whatsoever a man sows he will reap. Gal. 6:7

13. ETHICS OF DISCIPLESHIP AND SOUL-WINNING

The last word of every man before he leaves the world usually is the most strongest and important word as Jesus said to His own in Matthew 28:19-20 that

Go ye therefore, and teach all nations, baptizing them in the name of the Father, and of the Son, and of the Holy Ghost:

Teaching them to observe all things whatsoever I have commanded you: and, lo, I am with you always, even unto the end of the world. Amen.

Anything the church is doing that is not leading to soul winning and discipleship is just a mere funfair or jamboree. This ethics of the great commission must be commissioned in our daily work with God. This must be done daily and Jesus gave us the utmost assurance of divine security even in this wicked world that "... *and, lo, I am with you always, even unto the end of the world. Amen".*

The love of many Christians concerning evangelism and discipleship is growing cold and in our very eyes, our inheritance are being taken over by other religion without any hesitation.
Jesus said ...
Nevertheless when the

> *Anything the church is doing that is not leading to soul winning and discipleship is just a mere funfair or jamboree.*

Son of man cometh, shall he find faith on the earth? Luke 18:8. Shall HE find faith in evangelism in people?

14. ETHICS OF MINISTERING WITH POWER.

Nothing changes in life until power or force is applied. Ministry follows the same pattern even Jesus Christ the custodian of grace and power said in Gospel according to Saint John 4:48 that 'Except ye see signs and wonders, ye will not believe'. Signs and wonder differentiate us in ministry and the type of result we get.
An apostle, a prophet, an evangelist, a pastor, a teacher, a bishop or a church worker who

ministers without power in Christ is not different from a mere lecturer in the classroom or a motivational speaker.

You cannot make a meaningful impart in ministry without the use of the power of God. Apostle Paul, a saint of notable results said

> *For the kingdom of God is not in word, but in power. 1Cor. 4:20*

> *And my speech and my preaching was not with enticing words of man's wisdom, but in demonstration of the Spirit and of power: 1Cor. 2:4.*

To get power of God is free but it's not cheap. You have prices to pay such as: prayer, holy living, fasting, giving, meditation, worship etc.

15. ETHICS OF LIVING OR MINISTERING JOYFULLY.

Joy is the inner courage to win daily battles. Joy is contagious and anyone around joy will be implicated. When joy is missing in the church or in a pastor's life, then regular defeat in every sphere is imminent. Joy which is a fruit of the Spirit can only be gotten in the Holy Spirit; it is also the antidote of life combats. Why does the Bible say in Philippians 4:4 **'Rejoice in the Lord always:**

and again I say, Rejoice'? Because the joy of the Lord is your strength. Neh. 8:10. If you are not joyful in the Holy Ghost, you cannot excel in ministry. In ministry, there are hundreds and thousands of battles to fight depending on your calling. It takes joy the producer of strength to win all.

> *If thou faint in the day of adversity, thy strength is small. Proverb 24:10*

As a church leader, most people who come for counseling and prayers are sad. It is therefore, the joy you carry which is your strength that is their solutions.

> *A merry heart doeth good like a medicine: but a broken spirit drieth the bones. Proverb 17:22*

16. ETHICS OF HAVING GOOD MARRIAGE/HOME.

A billionaire or a politician or a lecturer or any professional can do well in their careers without a good marriage **BUT not a pastor**. A preacher or a church leader that has a good home or marriage will have very great chances to have a good congregation. This also involves raising good children for the Lord. This is what Paul the Apostle was talking about in 1Tim. 3:4-5 when he was listing the characteristics of a Bishop who is a church leader or a senior pastor to other pastors.

> *4: One that ruleth well his own house, having his children in subjection with all gravity;*
> *5: (For if a man know not how to rule his own house, how shall he take care of the church of God?)*

A Pastor with a scattered home or a divorcee or found in adultery, fornication and other sexual scandals is not qualified to lead congregation. What would he teach the people about marriage or marital

> *A billionaire or a politician or a lecturer or any professional can do well in their careers without a good marriage BUT not a pastor.*

relationship? Should he/she teach the congregation scattered home, how to be a divorcee or how to live in the error of immorality? This is the problem! Some church leaders are even hidden or public polygamous. *Abomination!*

My submission is this, besides ethics 24 above, 'ethics of studying and knowing church history' is very good but as a church leader, if you don't know the history of your father, mother, father-in-law or mother-in-law's marriage and if they were divorcee or polygamous, you might be a victim of divorce, polygamy and all kinds sexual scandals. This does not respect being anointed; it is an evil pattern that you must contend with deliberately in the spirit because they are already in the gene of the family.

Let us see father Abraham in the Bible as an example, a friend of God and yet he and his children could not escape some evil patterns not handled. And they also experience some good pattern because it was in their gene.

1. **Second Born Being made the First Born of the House.**
   ➤ Isaac versus Ishmael. Gen. 17:20-21.
   ➤ Jacob versus Esau. Gen. 25:23, Gen. 25:32-34
   ➤ Ephraim versus Manasseh. Gen.48:13-20

2. **They all married to beautiful wives**
   ➤ Abraham Gen. 12:11
   ➤ Isaac Gen. 26:7
   ➤ Jacob Gen. 29:17-18

3. **Entering into troubles because of beautiful wives.**
   ➤ Abram. Gen. 12:14-15
   ➤ Isaac. Gen. 26:7-9
   ➤ Jacob Gen.29:20-25

4. **Delay in child bearing**
   ➤ Abraham Gen. 16:1-2
   ➤ Isaac Gen. 25:21
   ➤ Jacob Gen. 29:31

5. **Being polygamous in marriage.**
   ➤ Abram married Sarah, Hagar and Ketura. Gen. 16:1-3, Gen. 25:1

- ➢ Isaac escaped this pattern
- ➢ Jacob inherited same and did more than Abraham. Married Leah, Rachel, Zilpah and Bilhah. Gen. 29:18-30

6. <u>They went down to Egypt because of famine</u>
- ➢ Abraham Gen. 12:10
- ➢ Isaac almost went down to Egypt left for divine caution. Gen. 26:1-2
- ➢ Jacob/Israel Gen. 42: 3, and Gen. 46:3-6

7. <u>They all lied at one point or the other.</u>
- ➢ Abraham lied to the King of Egypt. Gen. 12:12-18.
- ➢ Isaac lied to Abimelech king of Philistine. Gen. 26:6-7
- ➢ Jacob lied to Isaac Gen.27:19
- ➢ Jacob/Israel children lied to their father over Joseph matter. Gen.37:31-36
- ➢ Joseph was lied against by Potiphar's wife. Gen. 39:14

<u>My Advice:</u>
Oh Man and Woman of God, please do everything possible in the Lord to keep your marriage safe from evil patterns of your family strange

> *Good marriage opens doors for good ministry!*
>
> *If heaven is not the ultimate reason for our living, then it is very profound that we are of all men most miserable.*

and

environmental influences. Safe your home from

ministerial reproaches; and no matter how busy you are for the Lord, attend to your children issues early so that God would be glorified in them. Remember good marriage opens doors for good ministry!

17. ETHICS OF LOOKING FORWARD TO ETERNITY IN HEAVEN.

As servants of God, no matter what we are doing on earth in the course of preaching the gospel, if heaven is not the ultimate reason for our living, then it is very profound that we are of all men most miserable.

If in this life only we have hope in Christ, we are of all men most miserable. 1Cor. 15:19".

Whether we like it or not; whether we know it or not; whether we believe it or not, Jesus will come back again. The Bible says when He shall appear, we shall be like Him. Everyone truly expecting Jesus must keep himself pure as He is. 1John 3:2-3.

> *2: Beloved, now are we the sons of God, and it doth not yet appear what we shall be: but we know that, when he shall appear, we shall be like him; for we shall see him as he is.*
>
> *3: And every man that hath this hope in him purifieth himself, even as he is pure.*

No matter how anointed you are, every man and woman of God called into ministry must leave the work one day either by a way of death or by rapture. Therefore, put in your best in obedience before the time so that your rewards could be massive.

> *I must work the works of him that sent me, while it is day: the night cometh, when no man can work. John 9:4.*

Also, remember we brought nothing to this world and it is very certain that we shall take nothing away. So take life easy!

> *6: But godliness with contentment is great gain.*
> *7: For we brought nothing into this world, and it is certain we can carry nothing out.*
> *8: And having food and raiment let us be therewith content. 1Tim. 6:6-8.*

CHAPTER FOUR

ETHICS OF INVITING GUEST- SPEAKERS

Sometimes, external ministers can be invited to preach for you especially in the area of ministry you don't have capacity for. But there are basic things to put in place for things to be alright. Let us consider some of them.

1. **MAKE SURE THERE IS NEED FOR THE INVITATION**
   You may invite a man of God in the area of ministry you don't have capacity for. For example, a prophet may invite a teacher to teach God's word because he is not a teacher. A pastor may embark on serious soul winning drive by inviting an evangelist. It is all about ministerial synergy!

2. **MAKE SURE THE INVITED GUEST IS GENUINE MINISTER OF GOD**
   You must invite a genuine man of God for all your programmes where necessary, the reason for this is that more problems would not be created for you after his/her departure. Always invite a man/woman you know.

3. **AS AN INVITED GUEST, DON'T TAKE THE ADVANTAGE OF YOUR HOST**

There are invited guests who would be looking for the church members' contacts especially the rich ones so that he or she could call them even after the programme is over. If the members called you, refer them to the man who invited you in order not to create distrust.

Many ministers of the gospel have lost tangible contacts in ministry because of this error of looking out for their hosts' rich contacts. Avoid it!

4. **MAKE SURE YOUR GUEST SPEAKER IS NOT AFTER MONEY OR A LOVER OF MONEY**

The birds of the same feather flock together. If you are not a lover of money, you will not invite a lover of money as pastor to your congregation.

10: For the love of money is the root of all evil: which while some coveted after, they have erred from the faith, and pierced themselves through with many sorrows.

11: But thou, **O man of God**, flee these things; and follow after righteousness,

godliness, faith, love, patience,
meekness. 1Tim:6:10-11

5. MAKE SURE HE/SHE IS NOT A SELF-PROMOTER BUT GOD'S

When a man who always talk about himself with the 'I' 'I' 'I' consciousness and mentality is invited, be very sure that he would leave self on your pulpit at his departure. When you see a minister like this, don't invite him no matter his or her title and the 'fire' he/she carries or vomit. By their fruit we shall know them.

6. MAKE SURE AS HOST YOU TAKE CARE OF YOUR INVITED GUEST WELL

If you don't have money to spend before initiating a programme, wait till you get money before giving out invitation to your proposed guests except it is an agreement between two of you that he or she is coming to preach because you have been friends for years. Or as a way for the work to grow when the guest knows that the financial capacity of the church is very low.

7. IF YOUR INVITED GUEST IS A SENIOR MINISTER TO YOU, MAKE SURE YOU RECEIVE HIM YOURSELF

When you are inviting a senior minister of the gospel, please make sure you receive him yourself at the Airport or the Park as a way of according him honour because honour should be given to whom it is due.

8. GIVE YOUR INVITED GUEST SPEAKER GOOD HONORARIUM ACCORDING TO YOUR CAPACITY

➢ Give your guest speaker honorarium according to your financial ability.

➢ Don't do programme and end up in debt as this may turn against the host later.

➢ If he/she raises fund, make sure there is need in the church for the fund raised.

➢ The honorarium should not be based on the percentage of fund raised or with a specific sharing formula. That could tear fellowship apart and God hates it.

9. MAKE SURE YOUR GUEST SPEAKERS IS NOT A NOVICE

Your guest speaker should not be a novice in the things of God but a mature minister in faith. They must not have or use sarcastic language on the altar or must not be a man that is intoxicated with little level of achievements. Rather invite a man/woman with large heart and humility.

Not a novice, lest being lifted up with pride he fall into the condemnation of the devil. 1Tim. 3:6

10. AS INVITED GUEST, MAKE SURE YOU SAY GOOD THINGS ABOUT YOUR HOST ELSE YOU MAY NOT BE INVITED AGAIN

No matter the age of the host to the guest or the age of the guest to the host, the guest must as a necessity respect the host and say good things about him when around. That has a lot to say about the guest. Failure to do this may block the guest's way in future.

11. LET THE PURPOSE OF THE PROGRAMME TO HOLD BE FOR SOULS

We are in the generation where nearly every programme held in many churches is for money; the primary purpose of the programme to hold should be for souls' salvation, restoration, deliverance, healing etc and not for money except the programme is tagged fund-raising to meet specific needs in the church.

12. Let all things done glorify Jesus!

CHAPTER FIVE

ETHICS OF PASTORS OVER CONGREGATIONS

Leading a Church is one of the exciting things in ministry but can also be a great nightmare if not done properly as frustration might set in which would jeopardize the success of the job already put in place.

1. Everyone called to lead a congregation should know that it is a privilege and not a right. Therefore, every member of the congregation should be treated with utmost respect.

2. Everyone called to lead a congregation should know that human behavioural studies are necessary and required to succeed. In other words, if you don't understand those you're leading by taking precautions to your leadership styles, they might lead you out of your calling. Moses listened too much to the people's complaints, he was distracted and was sent out of ministry early. Num 20: 1-12.

3. Church leaders should not always think about what they can get from the congregation, they should also look at what they can do for the congregation because in solving congregations' problems, pastors' problems would be solved.

4. Church/congregation leadership ethics should be of Shepherd and sheep relationship. A

Shepherd must protect and provide spiritual food and guide for the sheep so that the congregation should not experience spiritual malnutrition, dehydration and kwashiorkor.

5. Preaching responsibilities of a pastor require adequate time to prayer and preparation, so that the presentation will be biblically based, theologically correct, and clearly communicated.

6. Pastors (shepherds) who cannot or who has lost what it takes to feed the congregation spiritually and guide them in the way of God is advised to resign from such assignment because it is better you don't do it at all than doing it wrongly.

7. Every pastor should know that misleading God's people is a capital offense in the Court of heaven and that it attracts punishment.

8. Pastoral counseling should be maintained confidentially strict, except in cases where disclosure is necessary to prevent harm to persons and/or is required by law. Counseling discussion should not surface in the pastor's next sermons.

9. Every pastor should seek to be a servant-minister of the church by following the example of Christ in faith, love, wisdom, courage, and integrity.

CHAPTER SIX

ETHICS OF A LEADING PASTOR AND ASSOCIATE/ASSISTING PASTORS

This ethics are found in the several pages of the Holy Bible with the men of old;
Moses/Aaron
Moses/Joshua
Elijah/Elisha
Jesus Christ/Apostles

Every pastor either Head of a congregation or General Overseers of a ministry as the case may be or those assisting them have their roles to play in ensuring good result over the congregations and the ministries.

In my Christian life of about 30 years old, I have seen serious disorderliness, greed, anarchy and controversies among Senior and junior pastors.

Therefore, in my opinion, I will advise that there should be a working document in form of code of conduct or policies which would be a guide of operation and states the duties of both the leading (senior) and the assisting pastors in their Churches. I will talk more on the assistance/associate pastors in this chapter because most problems in pastoral setting come from them:

1. The very responsibilities of every minister either leading or assisting pastors in the hierarchical

order under in every ministry should be clearly defined.

2. Every assisting pastor should assist faithfully.

3. Every leading pastor should lead faithfully and reliably.

4. Every assisting pastor should know his/her boundary in duties execution.

5. Every assisting pastor should not be rebellious against the constituted authority. Rom. 13:1-2

6. Every assisting or associate pastor should not have empire under the leading pastor as this is a way of sponsoring division in the Church. 2 Sam. 15:22

7. Every assisting or associate pastor should respect, honour and project their leading pastors.

8. Every assisting or associate pastor should know that whatsoever a man sows he/she reaps. Gal. 6:7. Some Senior pastors are crying today even in the midst of blessings because they are reaping the evils they did when they were Assistant/Associate pastors to Senior pastors. Be warmed!

9. Every leading or Senior pastor should not be threatened at the gifting of the

associate/assisting pastors. Or serve as oppressor to the junior pastors at the instance of their gifting. If senior pastors are humble enough, they will discover that such gifts will be very useful to them. Don't be intimidated. The senior pastors still have what the junior pastors don't have.

10. Every leading pastor should not be greedy of material things as this can set pastoral folds in confusion. When assistant or associate pastors see that the leading pastors always go home with church offerings or spend church offerings and tithes recklessly when their families are hungry; you can be very sure that such pastoral union will not last as the assistant and associate pastors will soon rebel.

11. All leading pastors should care for the assistant or associate pastors and lead with good examples, and should not be autocratic or tyrannic in operation.

YOU ARE BLESSED!

CHAPTER SEVEN

ETHICS OF RESIGNATION

By the rules of life, no one is designed to permanently stay on a job or in a place; that's what we don't pray for as human. However, there are hat guide the way one quits a job. There's a maxim that 'the way you close a door would determine if you could still use the door in future'. Every employee and employer must take caution the way appointments are terminated else it may close chapter of good existing relationship and cost either party severe future loss.

Let's consider the following fact before resignation in effected in church offices either on the part of administrative staff or the clergies.

1. **IF YOU WANT TO RESIGN, PLEASE RESIGN ALONE.**
   Resignation should be a personal issue, not a general or a group issue. When a key staff is resigning his position, he/she should not influence other staff to follow him/her.

2. **IF YOU MUST RESIGN, PLEASE DO IT PROFESSIONALLY AND HONOURABLY.**
   It is very expedient that every staff who wants to leave should leave professionally and decently especially in the face of crisis and when politics is involved. This could mar the future relationship of the employer and the employee.

3. **IF YOU WANT TO RESIGN, LET IT BE FOR A BETTER OFFER AS A CAREER BUILDER.**

This is a counsel for the church administrative or ministerial staff; don't just resign because the pay is small while you have nothing at stake to rest on, every experience acquired counts. God's leading and direction supersedes our emotions.

4. **MAKE SURE YOU GIVE ENOUGH TIME OF NOTICE.**
Every church should have working policy concerning appointments and resignations of staff which should be stated in the staff employment offer. Regardless of the terms of appointment, sufficient time of notice should be given by either party or pay in lieu of notices so that the position could be filled officially and appropriately in order to avoid vacancy.

5. **MAKE SURE THE EMPLOYER ACCEPTS YOUR RESIGNATION BEFORE YOUR DEPARTURE.**
We see today in most churches that either party may say 'your job is over or I am leaving now'. This can only happen in a disorganized setting. As employee, make sure that the concerned church authority accepts your resignation after giving due notice before your departure.

6. **DO PROPER HANDLING OVER EXERCISE FOR EASY WORK CONTINUITY.**
The way this is done shows how reliable and responsible an employee or employer is in duties execution. Before employees leave the employment finally, all items major or minor in their custody should be officially handed over to the incoming

officer or any appropriate designated officer in order to close unnecessary gap in the church operation.

7. **AS EMPLOYEES, PAY UP ALL YOUR DEBTS IF ANY.**

When a staff is leaving an employment with unpaid debt either as loan or other form of advances, they should be fully settled, except it is cancelled at the employer's prerogative. If there are entitlements for the staff, they should be set off against the debts.

8. **AS EMPLOYERS, GIVE YOUR STAFF DUE COMPENSATION THEY ARE ENTITLED TO GET.**

One of the ways to honour staffs' efforts is to pay them their due compensation at resignation.

1Timothy 5:18 says '*...Thou shalt not muzzle the ox that treadeth out the corn. And, The labourer is worthy of his reward*'.

Church employment should be a place where peaceful work is practiced NOT an establishment launched into a chaos.

CHAPTER EIGHT

BOOK SUMMARY

1. Ethics refers to well-based standards of right and wrong that prescribe what humans ought to do, usually in terms of duties, principles, specific virtues, or benefits to society. In other words, ethics implies a broader range of expected behaviors 8hand reflection about what should be done.

2. When violation of moral standard of life is exhibited in any society, all we see is moral atrocity among the children, teenagers and adults. For example, moral misconducts cause series of hindrances to full life attainments such as;
   - Loss of value,
   - Loss of reputation,
   - Loss of focus,
   - Loss of direction
   - Abuse of nature
   - Loss of original identity and
   - Ultimately moral crashing.

3. There is a very high level of moral decadence in our society including the church offices and pulpits; the church is experiencing an ethical free fall because of the behavior of her leaders. This has become an embarrassment to all Christians.

4. The Basic Administrative Ethics include

1. Ethics of Confidentiality
2. Ethics of Transparency
3. Ethics of creativity
4. Attending to Mails Regularly
5. Ethics of sincerity in all things
6. Ethics of proper planning
7. Ethics of separation of account (Entity Concept)
8. Ethics of leading with visionary approach
9. Ethics of depending on the Holy Spirit for divine wisdom for operation
10. Ethics of Proper Reporting
11. Ethics of operating professionally in every sphere
12. Ethics of periodic assessment of the ministry and administrative operations
13. Ethics of accountability of all delegated authority
14. Ethics of self-development in office or personal development
15. Ethics of maintaining proper filling system
16. Ethics of not skipping disciplinary actions for anybody
17. Ethics of providing regular training for office staff.
18. Ethics of Leading with Examples
19. Ethics of delegating authority properly and the accompanied responsibilities
20. Ethics of not owing staff monthly salary and other allowances.
21. Ethics of following hierarchy in order to get the organization structure straight

22. Ethics of avoiding church politics.

23. Ethics of regarding the government laws in operating the church.

24. Ethics of studying and knowing church history.

25. Ethics of studying the reasons people leave the church.

26. Ethics of appreciating pastors for their good works.

27. Ethics of preparing for staffs retirement

28. The ethics of time management in all we do.

29. Ethics of disagreeing with the spirit of Absalom (Rebellion)

30. Ethics of fund-raising

31. Ethics of not working in the church because of money.

32. Ethics of taking rest when the need arises in order to work more for the days ahead.

33. Ethics of using the best hand to lead the organizational roles.

34. Ethics of handling church conflicts as early as possible so that it won't degenerate into crisis.

35. Ethics of checks and balances.

36. Ethics of preparing meeting agenda before it holds.

37. Ethics of counseling without being bias or sentimental.

5. The basic ministerial ethics
    1. Ethics of focus

2. Ethics of truthfulness of the messages preached
3. Ethics of ministering without greed
4. Ethics of competence
5. Ethics of depending on the Holy God for the Ministerial establishment.
6. Don't go into the ministry you don't have capacity and Grace for
7. Ethics of adequate preparation before preaching or teaching
8. Ethics of living in harmony with and among co-ministers
9. Ethics of accountability
10. Ethics of giving respect to those who are ahead in ministry.
11. Ethics of commending or lifting one another up publicly.
12. Ethics of helping one another in time of trouble.
13. Ethics of Discipleship and Soul-winning.
14. Ethics of ministering with power.
15. Ethics of living or ministering joyfully.
16. Ethics of having good marriage.
17. Ethics of looking forward to eternity in heaven.
18. Ethics of inviting Guest Speakers.

6. Ethics of inviting guest- speakers.

1. Make sure there is need for the invitation.
2. Make sure the invited guest is genuine minister of God.

3. As an invited Guest, don't take the advantage of your host.
4. Make sure your guest speaker is not after money or a lover of money.
5. Make sure he/she is not a self-promoter but God's.
6. Make sure as host you take care of your invited guest well.
7. If your invited guest is a Senior minister to you, make sure you receive him yourself
8. Give your invited Guest Speaker good honorarium according to your capacity.
9. Make sure your Guest Speakers is not a novice.
10. As invited Guest, make sure you say good things about your host else you may not be invited again.
11. Let the purpose of the programme to hold be for souls.

7. Ethics of pastors over congregations
    1. Everyone called to lead a congregation should know that it is a privilege and not a right.
    2. Everyone called to lead a congregation should know that human behavioural studies are necessary and required to succeed.
    3. Church leaders should not always think about what they can get from the congregation, they should also look at what they can do for the congregation.

4. Church/congregation leadership ethics should be of Shepherd and sheep relationship.
5. Preaching responsibilities of a pastor require adequate time to prayer and preparation, so that the presentation will be biblically based, theologically correct, and clearly communicated.
6. Pastors (shepherds) who cannot or who has lost what it takes to feed the congregation spiritually and guide them in the way of God is advised to resign.
7. It is better you don't do pastoral work at all than doing it wrongly
8. Every pastor should know that misleading God's people is sin.
9. Counseling discussion should not surface in the pastor's next sermons.
10. Every pastor should seek to be a servant-minister of the church

8. Ethics of a leading pastor and associate/assisting pastors

1. The very responsibilities of every minister in the hierarchical order should be clearly defined in form of code of conduct or policies.
2. Every assisting pastor should assist faithfully.
3. Every leading pastor should lead faithfully and reliably.
4. Every assisting pastor should know his/her boundary in duties execution.

5. Every assisting pastor should not be rebellious against the constituted authority. Rom. 13:1-2
6. Every assisting or associate pastor should not have empire under the leading pastor as this is a way of sponsoring division in the Church.
7. Every assisting or associate pastor should respect, honour and project their leading pastors.
8. Every leading or Senior pastor should not be threatened at the gifting of the associate/assisting pastors.
9. Every leading pastor should not be greedy of material things as this can set pastoral folds in confusion.

9. **Ethics of Resignation**
   1. If you want to resign, please resign alone.
   2. If you must resign, please do it professionally and honourably.
   3. If you want to resign, let it be for a better offer as a career builder.
   4. Make sure you give enough time of notice.
   5. Make sure the employer accepts your resignation before your departure.
   6. Do proper handling over exercise for easy work continuity.
   7. As employees, pay up all your debts if any.
   8. As employers, give your staff due compensation they are entitled to get.

CHAPTER EIGHT

SPIRIT INSPIRED QUOTES FROM THIS BOOK BY THE AUTHOR.

1. There is a very high level of moral decadence in our society including the church offices and pulpits; the church is experiencing an ethical free fall because of the behavior of her leaders.
2. When plans are still being formulated, though yet to be finalized or approved and the leaders or administrators divulge them, then there is no administration in such a place
3. Openness or transparency in administration is a virtue that is missing in many churches today because of the shady deals of many church leaders.
4. A dull administrator or head of a church that cannot think fast or strategize church operations will only succeed in gathering dull people to himself.
5. Nothing is as painful as God is around to help His people by giving illuminative, tangible and result-oriented ideas, and the pastor or the administrator cannot discern that.
6. In executing projects for the church, taking of bribe in whatever that's being done in the office is a serious offence in the Court of Heaven
7. Nothing just happen on earth, they are planned and worked for.
8. Why must you not plan when God is a great planner?
9. Church moneys are the peoples sweat and sacrificial penny given for the furtherance of the gospel.

10. Vision as Creative imagination and the mental capacity to construct the future one desires and make it a reality is an ethic that must be lived with in our churches.
11. A ministry or church without vision will soon become a mission field for other visionary ministries or churches to explore'
12. Wisdom of God makes an ordinary man/woman do extraordinary things.
13. When wisdom of God is not in view in our church administrations, foolishness and stupid acts would be our watchwords and targets. Wisdom of God is a key to life.
14. Engineer who downplays on the professional ethics of building may lose his license and incur great loss (loss of human, money and other valuable resources) for the church if the building collapsed.
15. My counsel to all professionals who God has called to serve in the church is that instead of the church members and authorities to force them into shortcut that would have them being blamed at the end, they should resign from that work until the balance is struck, before the whole world would see them as a big fool.
16. Periodic assessment of general operational strategies and base is a must in the church if we must move forward with salient performances and glorify God
17. When records are lost or missed up easily in any organization is a way to slow down the progress as no meaningful decisions can be made without records at hand.

18. As much as possible in the church, nobody should be a 'sacred cow' or tagged 'the untouchable' to thwart Disciplinary Committee (DC) decisions.
19. Everybody in the church administration should not be self-centered or selfish so that we would not bring up half-baked Christians for the Lord who would come and turn upside-down the good work we have done for the Lord.
20. If people in the other religions and in the Terrorist world can spend millions of dollars to advance their evil course in training their own; how much more the church of God which have a focus and Kingdom goals at heart?
21. Order is the mother of progress. Organization structure or hierarchical order is not for fun, it is for structural balance.
22. Serious minded people as church members walk away from visionless pastors and Administrators.
23. When the congregation honours their pastors, they are also honouring God in heaven.
24. *God gave all of us twenty four (24) hour every day, seven (7) days every week, four (4) weeks every month, twelve months (12) every year. What you do with your time depends on what your time will do to you*
25. What is needed in the church should be what to raise fund for and should be well accounted for.
26. pastors also should not hide under raising fund for church needs to raise fund for themselves, it's wrong.
27. Rest is medicinal. Rest is good health advocator. Rest is preparing for better work tomorrow.

28. Stress is a silent killer which causes chest pain, high cholesterol, cardiac (heart) problems, depression etc.
29. Stress can change temperament of gentle pastors as misplaced anger, and aggressions may be the results
30. Don't put a novice in the position of a professional. It's a big risk.
31. Checks and balances are not a sign of hatred or sentimental display of distrust but it has been the principle of achieving the best for every organization.
32. Don't be a superman counselor who fails before novice counselees because of saying what you don't know.
33. Focus is what guarantees your next success and achievement in ministry despite all odds.
34. No matter what you see, rejoice in the Lord always so that you can cause others to be joyful also.
35. Greed is eating one's tomorrow today. Greed is one of the vices that have stopped many ministers of the gospel untimely in ministry.
36. Ministry must be done with Holy Bible Curriculum, it is the work of the Holy God that must be done by holy people in the holy way.
37. You cannot help God in ministry! Other religions help their gods but in Christianity, our God helps us.
38. Doing ministry you don't have capacity and grace for is an act of pride.
39. One thing that is missing among the young ministers of today is that most of them don't know those who are ahead of them in ministry

40. We are in the era where the challenge or problem encountered by a minister makes other ministers to celebrate instead of interceding with them.
41. An apostle, a prophet, an evangelist, a pastor, a teacher, a bishop or a church worker who ministers without power in Christ is not different from a mere lecturer in the classroom or a motivational speaker.
42. To get power of God is free but it's not cheap. You have prices to pay such as: prayer, holy living, fasting, giving, meditation, worship etc.

CHAPTER NINE

REVISION TESTS

1. Define Ethics
2. List and explain twenty administrative ethics.
3. List and explain ten ministerial ethics.
4. What are the basic things which must be considered before bringing in an invited guest?

CHAPTER TEN

PRAYER POINTS

1. Holy Spirit of God, shape my behaviors to your taste.
2. In the name of Jesus, I will not use my hand to punish myself in ministry.
3. Power of the Highest, manifest in my calling.
4. The grace to do ministry according to God's grace, I receive in Jesus name.
5. O Lord, in my life, in my calling and in my walk with You, let Your will be done in Jesus name.

BOOKS BY PASTOR APELORIOYE I. DAVID

❖ Victory over the Storms of Life

- ❖ Effective Church Administration (The making of the Holy Spirit) Volume 1

- ❖ Effective Church Administration (The making of the Holy Spirit) Volume 2

- ❖ Church Politics (The killer of Great Grace)

- ❖ Victory over Untimely Death in Ministry.

- ❖ The Ministry Of Assistant And Associate Pastors

- ❖ Fundamental Church Administrative And Ministerial Ethics

- ❖ Salvation And Sanctification (The Foundation Of Our Christian Walk)

- ❖ The Journey of a Backslider (From Jerusalem to Jericho)

- ❖ Journey to Expansion and Settlement

- ❖ The Call to Ministry

- ❖ The Messenger Without A Message.

- ❖ Church Accounting

- ❖ Capacity Building (The Focus Of This Generation)

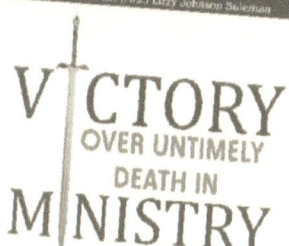

ABOUT THE BOOK

The ethics in this book are set out very clearly in order to enhance our administrative and ministerial productivity of the church. Ethics implies a broader range of expected behaviors and reflection about what should be done. For persons who work in church as nonprofit organizations, duty has a special importance if we must continue to enjoy good will.

There is a very high level of moral decadence in our society including the church offices and pulpits; the church is experiencing an ethical free fall because of the behavior of her leaders.

This has become an embarrassment to all Christians. Administrative and Ministerial Ethics address this issue and offer clear, candid, and comprehensive helps to both Pastors, Church Administrators, Secretaries, Committees and members.

ABOUT THE AUTHOR:

Pastor Apelorioye Igbekeleoluwa David is a called Evangelist and a teacher of the God's word. He ministers in Churches, Conferences, Seminars, and Crusades both locally and internationally under the deep unction of the Holy Spirit for the liberation of souls into God's Kingdom.

He is a Chartered Management Accountant and a Chartered Administrator and a member of Association of Forensic and Investigative Auditors; he holds MBA in Finance and M. Sc. in Social Work from the renown Ladoke Akintola University of Technology, Ogbomoso. Nigeria. Also he a graduate of The Redeemed Christian Bible College (RCBC), School of Disciple and Omega Bible Institute.

Presently he is serving as the Church Administrator of Omega Fire Ministries with the International Headquarters in Auchi, Edo State, Nigeria. A ministry ordained by God with the core Mission as revealed to the President/ Founder Apostle Professor Johnson Suleman. Thus "wipe out tears, restore people to their destinies, through the revelation of the word, manifestation of power and the reality of the Holy Spirit".

He is happily married to Pastor (Mrs.) Odion Deborah Apelorioye and is blessed with four children.